21125r
599.3r
V06

Are You My Rabbit?

by Julia Vogel
Illustrated by Matthew Williams

Content Consultant:
Gerald Brecke
Doctor of Veterinary Medicine

Are You My Pet?

visit us at www.abdopublishing.com

Published by Magic Wagon, a division of the ABDO Publishing Group, 8000 West 78th Street, Edina, Minnesota 55439. Copyright © 2009 by Abdo Consulting Group, Inc. International copyrights reserved in all countries. All rights reserved. No part of this book may be reproduced in any form without written permission from the publisher.

Looking Glass Library™ is a trademark and logo of Magic Wagon.

Printed in the United States.

Text by Julia Vogel
Illustrations by Matthew Williams
Edited by Jill Sherman
Interior layout and design by Emily Love
Cover design by Emily Love

Library of Congress Cataloging-in-Publication Data
Vogel, Julia.
 Are you my rabbit? / by Julia Vogel ; illustrated by Matthew Williams ; content consultant, Gerald Brecke.
     p. cm. — (Are you my pet?)
 Includes index.
 ISBN 978-1-60270-245-5
 1. Rabbits—Juvenile literature. I. Williams, Matthew, 1971- ill. II. Title.
 SF453.2.V64 2009
 636.932'2—dc22
                                             2008003626

Note to Parents/Guardians:
This book can help you teach your child how to be a kind, responsible rabbit owner. But a child cannot handle all the responsibilities of having a pet, so we are glad that you will oversee your rabbit's care. Neutering or spaying your rabbit will help reduce pet overpopulation and make your rabbit healthier and happier. For your child's safety, adults should take primary care of cage cleaning and remind the child to wash hands after handling any pet.

Table of Contents

Is a Rabbit the Right Pet for Me?	4
Should My Rabbit Be Big or Small?	7
What Kind of Rabbit Would Be Best?	8
How Old Should My Rabbit Be?	10
What Does My Rabbit Need?	12
What Should I Feed My Rabbit?	16
How Do I Get to Know My Rabbit?	18
How Do I Teach My Rabbit?	23
How Do I Keep My Rabbit Safe?	24
How Do I Stay Safe?	28
Words to Know	30
Further Reading	31
On the Web	31
Index	32

Is a Rabbit the Right Pet for Me?

Do you like wiggly noses? Do you like petting soft fur? Do you like quiet, gentle play?

A rabbit takes a lot of care. Are you someone who can give a lot of care? A rabbit may be just the pet for you!

Pet Fact:
Pet rabbits are not like the wild rabbits in your yard. Never try to tame a wild rabbit!

Should My Rabbit Be Big or Small?

Some rabbits grow big, such as Flemish Giants. Some rabbits stay small, such as Mini Rexes. All rabbits need space to live and play. Big rabbits need more space. Small rabbits need less space.

Pet Fact:

There are more than 40 kinds, or breeds, of rabbits.

What Kind of Rabbit Would Be Best?

Different breeds of rabbits can have long fur or short fur. They can also have tall ears or floppy ears. Some are calm and gentle, such as English Lops. Some are excitable, such as Netherland Dwarfs. Some are friendly and easy to handle, such as Dutch rabbits.

Your parents can help you pick your rabbit. So can books and Web sites. Animal shelters take care of animals without homes. People there can help you pick a rabbit, too.

Pet Fact:

Baby rabbits are sometimes called bunnies. They are also called kits or kittens. Kits should stay with their moms until they are 8 weeks old.

How Old Should My Rabbit Be?

Baby rabbits, or bunnies, are cute! They need to chew—and chew and chew! They dash around and hide behind furniture.

Older rabbits still chew a lot, but they are calm. Bunnies may seem more fun at first, but adults can be easier to live with.

Pet Fact:

As soon as you get your rabbit, take it to the veterinarian.

What Does My Rabbit Need?

An outside rabbit needs a big hutch. Its roof stops the rain and the sides stop the wind. A nest box inside gives your rabbit a cozy place to sleep.

An inside rabbit needs a roomy cage. It should be big enough for the rabbit to stand up and stretch out. It is easier to keep a rabbit safe if it lives indoors.

A cage or hutch needs soft bedding. Bedding helps keep rabbits warm and comfy. Ripped newspaper or hay make good bedding. Shredded pine or cedar wood can make a rabbit sick.

All rabbits need outdoor play. Walk your rabbit on a leash or play together in a fenced pen. Never leave a pet rabbit alone in the yard.

Your rabbit will also need a dish for food and a bottle for water. Your rabbit will need a litter box, too. The litter box will be your rabbit's bathroom.

Pet Fact:

Rabbits like to stay clean. Put a litter box in a corner of the cage or hutch. Your rabbit will learn to use it.

What Should I Feed My Rabbit?

Rabbits love carrots. They love lots of other food, too. They need rabbit pellets and hay every day. A few raisins or an apple slice make good treats.

Feed your rabbit twice a day. Take your rabbit outside to eat clover. Make sure your rabbit has a stick to chew. Chewing keeps a rabbit's teeth healthy.

Pet Fact:

Keep your rabbit away from electrical cords. If a rabbit chews a cord, it could get hurt.

How Do I Get to Know My Rabbit?

At first your new rabbit may be shy. Let your rabbit rest for awhile. Speak softly and offer it a treat. Soon your rabbit will come out to play.

Watch how your rabbit looks. Then you can tell how your rabbit feels.

Is your rabbit hiding in a corner? That means your rabbit feels shy. Now is not the time to play.

Is your rabbit sniffing around? Are your rabbit's ears moving this way and that? That means your rabbit feels curious. It is time to play!

Is your rabbit stomping its back foot? That means your rabbit is scared. Do not pick it up. You might get scratched.

Pet Fact:
Rabbits have thin bones that break easily. Always pick your rabbit up with a hand under its bottom. Hold your rabbit close to your body.

How Do I Teach My Rabbit?

Your rabbit can learn many things. First, teach your rabbit to trust you. Always treat your rabbit with kindness. Speak softly, pet gently.

Teach your rabbit to come when you call. Call your rabbit's name. Offer your rabbit a treat when it comes. Your rabbit will learn fast.

Do not punish a rabbit for chewing your things. Keep things you do not want chewed away from your rabbit.

Pet Fact:
Do not hit your rabbit. Hitting does not teach.

How Do I Keep My Rabbit Safe?

Be careful about what you feed your rabbit. Wash fruit and vegetables before your rabbit eats them. Eating plants sprayed with chemicals can poison a rabbit. Potato plants, tomato plants, lettuce, spinach, cauliflower, cabbage, and some other plants can make your rabbit sick.

Weigh your rabbit. Check the pellet package to see how much to feed a rabbit that size. Too much food makes rabbits fat and unhealthy.

When you play outside, keep your rabbit inside a pen or on a leash. If a dog or cat comes near, your rabbit will be frightened. Take your rabbit inside.

Pet Fact:

*Rabbits love toys!
A place to dig is fun, too.
Ask your veterinarian for
a list of safe toys.*

How Do I Stay Safe?

Wash your hands after petting your rabbit or helping clean the cage. Do not pick up a scared rabbit. Instead, sit quietly beside your rabbit. Pet your rabbit's head and enjoy each other's company.

With love and care, a pet rabbit can live seven to twelve years. Enjoy this wonderful new friend for life!

Pet Fact:

Rabbits need grooming, or cleaning. Brush your rabbit's fur often. Help an adult clean your rabbit's cage every week. Ask your veterinarian to trim your rabbit's toenails.

Words to Know

animal shelter—a safe place for homeless animals.

bedding—shredded paper or other material lining an animal cage.

breed—a specific kind of animal within a species.

groom—to clean oneself to stay healthy.

hutch—an outdoor shelter for a rabbit.

litter box—a place where a rabbit goes to the bathroom.

train—to teach an animal rules or tricks.

veterinarian—an animal doctor.

Further Reading

Blackledge, Annabel. *Small Pet Care*. New York: DK Children, 2005.
Evans, Mark. *Rabbit: ASPCA Pet Care Guide*. New York: DK Children, 2001.
Fox, Sue. *Rabbit. Animal Planet Pet Care Library*. Neptune City, NJ: TFH Publications, 2006.
Gibbons, Gail. *Rabbits, Rabbits, & More Rabbits!* New York: Holiday House, 2001.

On the Web

To learn more about rabbits, visit ABDO Publishing Company on the World Wide Web at **www.abdopublishing.com**. Web sites about rabbits are featured on our Book Links page. These links are routinely monitored and updated to provide the most current information available.

Index

A
animal shelters 8

B
bedding 12, 15
bones 21
breeds 7, 8
bunnies 8, 10

C
cage 12, 15, 28
chewing 10, 16, 23
cleanup 28

D
Dutch rabbit 8

E
ears 8, 21
English Lop 8

F
Flemish Giant 7
food 15, 16, 24
fur 4, 8, 28

G
grooming 28

H
handling 18, 21, 23, 28
hiding 10, 18
hutch 12, 15

L
leash 15, 27
life span 28
litter box 15

M
Mini Rex 7

N
nest box 12
Netherland Dwarf 8

P
pens 15, 27
playing 4, 7, 15, 18, 21, 27

S
sickness 12, 24
size 7
sniffing 21

T
teaching 23
toys 27
treats 16, 18, 23

V
veterinarian 10, 27, 28

W
water 15
wild rabbits 4

Y
yard 4, 15